Contents

Grimoire

A PERSONAL—& MAGICAL—RECORD
✦✧ of ✧✦
Spells, Rituals, &
Divinations

ARIN MURPHY-HISCOCK
Author of
The Green Witch

Adams Media
New York   London   Toronto   Sydney   New Delhi

Aadamsmedia

Adams Media
An Imprint of Simon & Schuster, Inc.
100 Technology Center Drive
Stoughton, Massachusetts 02072

First Adams Media hardcover edition
October 2020

ADAMS MEDIA and colophon are trademarks of Simon & Schuster.

For information about special discounts for bulk purchases, please contact Simon & Schuster Special Sales at 1-866-506-1949 or business@simonandschuster.com.

The Simon & Schuster Speakers Bureau can bring authors to your live event. For more information or to book an event contact the Simon & Schuster Speakers Bureau at 1-866-248-3049 or visit our website at www.simonspeakers.com.

Interior design by Julia Jacintho
Interior images © 123RF/Stanislav Kharchevskyi

Manufactured in China

10 9 8 7 6 5 4 3

Library of Congress Cataloging-in-Publication Data
Names: Murphy-Hiscock, Arin, author.
Title: Grimoire / Arin Murphy-Hiscock, author of The Green Witch.
Description: First Adams Media hardcover edition. | Avon, Massachusetts: Adams Media, 2020. | Identifiers: LCCN 2020015815 | ISBN 9781507214244 (hc)

Subjects: LCSH: Witchcraft.
Classification: LCC BF1566 .M7885 2020 | DDC 133.4/3--dc23
LC record available at https://lccn.loc.gov/2020015815

ISBN 978-1-5072-1424-4

Contains material adapted from the following title published by Adams Media, an Imprint of Simon & Schuster, Inc.: *Spellcrafting* by Arin Murphy-Hiscock, copyright © 2020, ISBN 978-1-5072-1264-6.

Introduction

A grimoire is one of your most valuable tools and a way to truly make your practice personal and unique to your life and experiences. But where do you begin? What should you include? Fortunately, with *Grimoire* at your side, creating your own personal grimoire has never been easier.

Grimoire is not just another "how-to" grimoire book; rather, this book you hold in your hands IS your grimoire. Using this book, you will construct a personal grimoire that is truly reflective of you. Because starting a project of this magnitude can be a bit overwhelming, Part One will give you both basic knowledge and guidance on what you should include in your grimoire so you will have a starting point. In Part Two you'll find ample room to record your own spells, rituals, reflections, journal entries, and whatever else you feel is important to you and your practice. As you record your experiences, Part Two will transform into your own personal and individual grimoire!

Your grimoire is a reflection of your soul and spirituality; it is a private record and collection, not a universal one. This is why collecting only the work of others in your book leaves your practice one-dimensional. Messy though they may be, your dreams, hopes, flights of fancy, and attempts at spellcraft and ritual design are vital aspects of your spiritual development. Allow yourself the freedom to explore and experiment in your grimoire; it's a work in progress, just the way you are.

Starting a new grimoire is an exciting undertaking. There is so much potential ahead, so many discoveries to record, so much research to do and make notes on. There are explorations and experiments to be done. And there are responses and reflections to be made about your discoveries and experiences. Use this book as your spiritual tool and watch it grow and develop from the ground up just as your practice does!

How to Use This Book

This book serves two purposes: as inspiration for you as you start to pull together material for your own grimoire, and as a reference. The first part of this book contains material that can serve as the starting point for you, providing basic knowledge and information that are applicable to various witchcraft practices. The second part of the book provides plenty of space for you to add your own material.

How you use the first part of this book is up to you. If you're brand-new to your practice, reading through it will help you gain a basic grounding in the information frequently used in witchcraft and nature-based practice. If you already have a background, you can consult it when you're pulling together timing or correspondence information for a working. You can also use it as a template or guide when collating your own information to add to your grimoire. In short, it's a handy collection of basic reference material to use however you need.

Ultimately this book will contain a record of your early work along your path. Your grimoire is your most reliable resource for looking over previous work and evaluating your progress, evolution, and development. This is part of why it is vitally important for you to keep detailed and up-to-date records. Consistent use of your spiritual journal helps you organize all the bits of interesting information you discover on your path. It provides a concrete record of your work, so that you can understand where you might have gone wrong in spellcraft or ritual, or how to re-create successful rituals and spells. Overall, a well-maintained grimoire helps you keep your practice fresh, and helps you practice more efficiently. It is a tool, and a very valuable one.

Approaching Your Grimoire

There exist two general mindsets related to the magical journal. The first approach treats the grimoire as a polished final copy of all your work. Spells and rituals are copied into it only after they have been thoroughly perfected through practice.

The second approach treats the tool like a complete collection of all the spiritual work you do. It includes records and texts of rituals and spells (successes and failures); clearly annotated notes taken from books you've read; recipes for herbal concoctions you've tried and notes on the results; notes on meditations and dreams; divination records; correspondences; and so forth.

For many, a grimoire is more valuable when it encompasses the entire spectrum of the spiritual journey. If you note down only what works, you lose the benefit of being able to look back on your mistakes (one of the best ways to track your progress). It's nice to have a beautiful, formal version of your grimoire, but a spiritual journal is much more helpful in learning and growing if it contains records of your progress and thoughts as well.

It can be difficult for a spiritual person to accept that they weren't as advanced a few years ago, or even a few months ago. Denying one's past self is not a healthy thing to do when pursuing a spiritual path, however. Embracing your older records and work is to accept that you are an eternal seeker, and in constant evolution. Even after years of experience, we humbly acknowledge that there is always more to learn, and still deeper levels of our own souls to critically examine.

Remember, this book is not a manual for practice; it's a guide to creating your own grimoire. If you seek a more practical guide, please look at *Spell-crafting: Strengthen the Power of Your Craft by Creating and Casting Your Own Unique Spells*. You may also be interested in *The Green Witch* and *The House Witch*, both of which look at nature-based spirituality and working with the energies of the natural world.

Part One

Grimoire Basics

This part looks at the kind of knowledge you might want to include in your grimoire. It also provides some basic information that would be included in a beginner's grimoire, such as references for moon phases, festivals, common correspondences, and so forth. It offers you a chance to think about what you might want to record in your own grimoire, what format(s) you might want to use, and how much or how little information you might want to include in your correspondence records or research on various topics.

Together with the second half of this book—the part where you will collect your own material—this information constitutes the basis of a beginner's grimoire.

Book Blessing

A book blessing serves multiple intentions. It dedicates the grimoire to its purpose, which is to be a magical tool supporting your spiritual development. It's a manifesto of sorts, declaring your intention in using the book and your spiritual goals. It's also a mission statement, outlining the values you intend to uphold in this pursuit. It's a good thing to start off with in a brand-new book. You can put it on the first page or a couple of pages in, after whatever else you feel should come first.

A blessing can be as simple as a written invocation in the front of your grimoire. It can be an elaborate ritual in which you cleanse and bless your grimoire and dedicate it to the gods you follow. It may be a piece of art you create in sacred space to insert in your grimoire. As long as it's done with intention, your book blessing can be anything.

Here's a sample book blessing:

Grimoire,
Be for me the container of my secrets,
The aggregate of my knowledge,
The well of my inspiration.
May my work be blessed by you,
My records safely held,
And the knowledge an inspiration.

May you contain my energy safely,
Storing it against my future need,
And may the information you hold
Support me as I follow my path
And honor nature.

Book Protection Spell

Sometimes you want your grimoire to be protected, especially if you live or use it in a place that isn't hospitable to your spiritual path. Here's a spell to write into the front of your book to help defend it from unwanted abuse:

Book of secrets,
Be safe from prying eyes.
May those who seek to penetrate your
Mysteries be confounded,
Their intentions turned aside,
Their interest transformed to disinterest.

Be protected from those who would
Harm you,
And who threaten my security.
So may it be.

Wisdom of Your Path

Every grimoire should have a section for general information about your chosen path. This can include tenets, invocations, background, beliefs, and so forth. It also covers basic things that are called upon frequently in your practice, such as elemental information, circle casts and quarter calls (if you use them), techniques to charge or empower something, and directions on how to cleanse and purify an object. (In the following pages you'll find some general information on many of these items to use as reference.)

This section can also be a place to state your moral and ethical approach and express your feelings about your work as a witch, your feelings about nature, and your personal goals concerning your spiritual path.

This is also where you'll keep general information about your spiritual studies. For example, if you read an interesting chapter about meditation and there are some ideas you'd like to record, this is the place to do it.

Basic Correspondences

The energies of the four elements in Western occult tradition are:

◊ **Earth:** Stability, prosperity, abundance, wealth, growth, expansion, manifestation, birth and death, fertility, materialization, loyalty
  * Representations: Soil, plants, stones, salt
  * Cardinal direction: North

◊ **Air:** Mind, mental work, knowledge, abstract thought, inspiration, finding lost things, teaching and learning, memory, beginnings
  * Representations: Wind, fans, feathers, incense, clouds, breath
  * Cardinal direction: East

◊ **Fire:** Energy, sexuality, passion, love, authority, transformation, purification, healing, destruction, will, creativity, protection, courage, strength, power
  * Representations: Candles, sun, blood, flame, heat, bonfires, hearth fires
  * Cardinal direction: South

◊ **Water:** Subconscious mind, intuition, emotions, feminine fertility, marriage, friendship, happiness, dreams, sleep, healing, cleansing, purification, sorrow, reflection, psychic ability
  * Representations: Ice, rain, wells, seas, oceans, rivers, lakes, springs
  * Cardinal direction: West

Techniques for Purifying Components and Supplies

Here are some simple methods for clearing odd or extraneous energy from your supplies.

Purifying Herbs

Herbs can be purified before use with this simple process:

1. Center and ground.
2. Hold your hands over the herb.
3. Draw energy up from the earth. Let it flow down your arms to your hands and to the herb.
4. Say, "With this energy you are purified, cleared of anything not your own."
5. The herb is ready to be used.

You can store the herb after purifying it, but it's worth sensing the energy before you use it later to see if it needs to be purified again. Purify if you're in doubt; the process is quick and won't hurt.

Purifying Stones

Stones are useful elements in spellwork because they can be recycled by cleansing and purifying them. This removes any previous energy coded into them as well as any stray energy they have collected along the way. (Don't worry; it doesn't remove their native energy.) Once a stone has been cleansed, it's ready to be used as a blank slate again.

There are several ways to cleanse a stone.

◊ **Salt:** A good way to cleanse a stone is to bury it in a small dish of salt for at least a day, longer if you feel the stone has heavy programming or has collected a lot of junky energy. Use any kind of salt you have on hand. You might want to keep the more expensive salt for actual spellwork, though.

◊ **Earth:** Bury the stone in a small dish of earth for three or more days. Earth from your garden is fine, as is earth from a bag of potting soil. You can use a potted houseplant for this, marking the spot with a toothpick so you can locate the stone when it's time. However, choose another method if the stone contains a lot of negative energy; that energy will be absorbed by the earth (which is the point of using the earth to cleanse the stone), but it will in turn be absorbed from the earth into the houseplant.

◊ **Water:** Pour water in a dish and set the stone in it. Water is an excellent purifier. If you add a pinch of salt to it, it becomes even more powerful. However, if there's any metal attached to or within the stone, skip the salt and use pure water.

◊ **Sunlight and moonlight:** The easiest of the cleansing techniques involves setting your stone on a windowsill where the direct sunlight or moonlight will hit it. Judge how long to leave it according to how much cleansing you feel the stone needs. You can set the stone on a mirror to enhance the effect.

Sky Magic

So much of our spiritual inspiration comes from the sky. Connected to the earth, we lift our eyes and gaze into the unknown, seeking insight into mysteries. This section covers the various aspects of sky magic, including moon phases, solar phases, zodiac signs, and planetary energies.

The Moon

Lunar energy is one of the key energies used in witchcraft. Moon phases are among the most common methods by which magical work is planned and performed. The general rule is that attraction or growth magic is performed in the first half of the lunar month, when the moon appears to be increasing in the sky. Banishing or magic associated with decrease or reduction is performed in the second half of the cycle, when the moon appears to shrink away in the sky.

A full moon occurs when the moon is lit up in its entirety. People who don't cast spells often refer to the dark moon as the new moon, as it signifies the beginning of a new lunar cycle. However, magically the new moon is the first visible slim crescent in the evening sky, about three days into the lunar cycle.

◊ **New moon:** The very first sliver of moon seen in the sky is called the new moon. This is technically a couple of days into the cycle, but in relation to our perception of the moon, it qualifies as the beginning. The new moon is appropriately associated with beginnings, the seeds of something that will come to fruition later. It is a good time for setting intentions. It is also a good time to plant.

◊ **Waxing moon:** *Waxing* means "growing," and that is exactly what the moon seems to be doing in the first half of its cycle. As its light increases in the sky, the lunar energy shifts more to attraction, expansion, and growth. This is a time to do work on ongoing projects that need support in their development. Prosperity, creativity, and learning are all areas to work on during the waxing moon.

◊ **Full moon:** In general, the full moon is a great catch-all time to power your magical work. It is associated with fruition, success, and culmination. Full moon energy is excellent for blessings, confirmations, and rites of passage. It also carries powerful healing energy.

◊ **Waning moon:** *Waning* means "decreasing or fading away," and that's what our perception of the moon tells us is happening as the shadow of the earth passes across it. As the moon's light decreases, the energy it holds turns to energy sympathetic to decreasing, reducing, or banishing things.

◊ **Dark moon:** The dark moon is when the last crescent vanishes and there appears to be no moon in the sky. Dark moon energy is good for introspection, preparation for future work, and nourishing your spirit. Quiet, restorative self-care is a good thing to work on at this time.

As you might expect, the full and dark moons traditionally represent the extremes of lunar energy. This doesn't mean extremes of quantity of energy—the moon doesn't have more or less power at any time during its cycle. Traditionally, most Western cultures associate the sight of the moon waxing with creative power and the dark moon with destructive power. The terms *creative* and *destructive* do not impart a positive and negative value to the energy; they refer instead to two natural functions of the life process: growth and decay.

Moon Signs

Each sign has a different personality that affects the lunar (or solar) energy when the luminary is passing through it. For example, if your spell is to help you meet new people, then you might choose to cast it when the moon is in the sign of Libra, the sign associated with social issues. The lunar energy you use to power your spell will be enhanced with Libran energy. Here's a list of correspondences for the signs of the zodiac. The correspondences are applicable to the moon (and, of course, to the sun as well; see Sun Signs: The Zodiac further on in this section).

◊ **Aries energy** is good for new beginnings and action.

◊ **Taurus energy** is good for manifestation.

◊ **Gemini energy** is excellent for communication and intellectual pursuits.

◊ **Cancer energy** is associated with family and the home.

◊ **Leo energy** is good for success.

◊ **Virgo energy** is organized and practical.

◊ **Libra energy** is terrific for social issues.

◊ **Scorpio energy** is passionate and just.

◊ **Sagittarius energy** is associated with study.

◊ **Capricorn energy** is stable and good for business issues.

◊ **Aquarius energy** is excellent for issues involving groups of people.

◊ **Pisces energy** is associated with mysticism and spiritual evolution.

Sun: Daily Cycle

The sun's daily cycle offers you the opportunity to match up magical work with the most favorable time of day. The day begins with the dawn and moves to midday, through sunset, and then to midnight. Each of these four phases is associated with basic energies to add extra power to your spell:

◊ **Dawn:** origins, new beginnings, illumination, children

◊ **Midday:** energy, growth, creation, increase

◊ **Sunset:** decrease, banishment, resolution, maturation

◊ **Midnight:** endings, gestation, stability

From these four points, you can extrapolate other times during the day, such as midmorning or midafternoon.

The sun also has a yearlong cycle that is reflected by the seasons, which carry energies similar to the four phases of the daily cycle:

◊ **Spring:** origins, new beginnings, birth

◊ **Summer:** passion, activity, creation/destruction

◊ **Autumn:** transformation, farewells, nostalgia

◊ **Winter:** introspection, planning

Remember that if you work with seasonal solar energy, your probable date of manifestation will be calculated by the appropriate seasonal phase. For example, if you work a spell for new beginnings in spring, then look for slow growth in summer, and the first harvested rewards of the project in the fall.

Planetary Energy

Apart from the moon and the sun, there are plenty of heavenly bodies to draw upon to power your spells with various energies.

The days of the week are each associated with certain planetary energies. The following list gives you an idea as to what energies are associated with each day, which can help you pinpoint when to do an associated spell or ritual:

◊ **Sunday** is ruled by the Sun. It is associated with active male energy, power, leadership, authority, success, and sports.

◊ **Monday** is ruled by the Moon. It is associated with feminine receptive energy, travel, the sea, hunting, cycles, reproduction, dreams, and psychic work.

◊ **Tuesday** is ruled by Mars. It is associated with active energy, aggression, destruction, conquest, violence, animals, and male sexuality.

◊ **Wednesday** is ruled by Mercury. It is associated with learning, intellectual pursuits, communication, gambling, medicine and healing, commerce, deception, and theft.

◊ **Thursday** is ruled by Jupiter. It is associated with good fortune, growth, rites of passage, expansion, finances, career, and bureaucracy.

◊ **Friday** is ruled by Venus. It is associated with music, dance, the arts, social occasions, love, emotion, and female sexuality.

◊ **Saturday** is ruled by Saturn. It is associated with the past, aging, death, abstract thought, higher study, and agriculture.

Sun Signs: The Zodiac

The Western zodiac is a set of twelve constellations. Roughly every thirty days, the sun appears to move into a different constellation. What actually happens is that our orbit shows us different constellations at different times of year and the one at the zenith of the sky above is said to rule the personality of someone born while the sun appears to occupy that constellation.

Each zodiac sign is represented by the constellation's name or figure, is ruled by a planet or other luminary, and is ruled by an element. See the following list:

◊ **Aries (the Ram)** is ruled by Mars; its ruling element is fire.

◊ **Taurus (the Bull)** is ruled by Venus; its ruling element is earth.

◊ **Gemini (the Twins)** is ruled by Mercury; its ruling element is air.

◊ **Cancer (the Crab)** is ruled by the Moon; its ruling element is water.

◊ **Leo (the Lion)** is ruled by the Sun; its ruling element is fire.

◊ **Virgo (the Virgin)** is ruled by Mercury; its ruling element is earth.

◊ **Libra (the Scales)** is ruled by Venus; its ruling element is air.

◊ **Scorpio (the Scorpion)** is ruled by Mars and Pluto; its ruling element is water.

◊ **Sagittarius (the Archer)** is ruled by Jupiter; its ruling element is fire.

◊ **Capricorn (the Sea Goat)** is ruled by Saturn; its ruling element is earth.

◊ **Aquarius (the Water Bearer)** is ruled by Saturn and Uranus; its ruling element is air.

◊ **Pisces (the Fish)** is ruled by Neptune and Jupiter; its ruling element is water.

Festivals and Celebrations

Keeping a list of festivals and days for celebrations is another mainstay of a grimoire. This section is where you'd record rituals for these celebrations too. Don't get trapped by the idea that you need a new ritual every time you celebrate an annual event. Repeating a tried-and-true ritual creates resonance, something that is valuable in a spiritual practice that focuses on rhythms and cycles.

Esbats

Esbats are rituals that celebrate the moon and its phases. Refer back to the previous Sky Magic section to review the phases of the moon and their associated energies. People often think of esbats as solely full moon celebrations, but in actuality esbats celebrate the moon in any phase.

To use the lunar energy of the moon in any of its phases, you do not need to be working your ritual at a precise time when the moon is in the sky. Phases don't automatically switch from one aspect to the next like a traffic light changing; they slowly blend into each other. For magical purposes we usually consider the energy of a full or dark moon to encompass the day before and after, as well as the actual day the moon occurs in the indicated phase.

If celebrating the moon according to the seasons interests you, there are a variety of sets of names for the full moons associated with each month:

Month	Old English	Colonial American	American Indian (Cherokee)
January	Winter Moon	Wolf Moon	Cold Moon
February	Trapper's Moon	Storm Moon	Bony Moon
March	Fish Moon	Chaste Moon	Windy Moon
April	Planter's Moon	Seed Moon	Flower Moon
May	Milk Moon	Hare Moon	Planting Moon
June	Rose Moon	Dyan Moon	Green Corn Moon
July	Summer Moon	Mead Moon	Ripe Corn Moon
August	Dog Day's Moon	Corn Moon	Fruit Moon
September	Harvest Moon	Barley Moon	Nut Moon
October	Hunter's Moon	Blood Moon	Harvest Moon
November	Beaver Moon	Snow Moon	Trading Moon
December	Christmas Moon	Oak Moon	Snow Moon

Seasonal Celebrations: The Wheel of the Year

The Wheel of the Year is the annual cycle of holy days and seasonal festivals that modern pagans often follow. Whether you celebrate them all, just the four seasonal markers, or add other festivals drawn from the culture(s) you honor, these eight festivals, or sabbats, are a balanced cycle of celebrations drawn from western European practices.

Yule

◊ **December 20–23: when the sun passes into the sign of Capricorn**

The word *Yule* comes from the Norse *jól*, which was a feast with merrymaking to honor the gods and to encourage plenty and peace. Also referred to as Midwinter (because it falls between Samhain and Beltaine), Yule occurs on the astronomical date of the winter solstice, which means the date varies from year to year.

Many cultures associate the winter solstice with the rebirth of the sun and the return of the light after the days have grown shorter and the nights longer. From approximately this point onward, the sun will wax larger and brighter once again until Midsummer. Yule celebrates the joyful promise of new growth in the darkness of winter.

Imbolc

◊ **February 1–2: or when the sun reaches 15 degrees of Aquarius**

Imbolc, one of two sabbats associated directly with a specific deity, is a festival to celebrate the beginning of spring. (Imbolc's partner across the Wheel is Lughnassadh, the Feast of Lugh.)

The modern eclectic pagan perception of Imbolc comes from three very different festivals. Imbolc is celebrated from sundown on February 1 to sundown on February 2 and is an agricultural festival marking the lambing and calving season in the British Isles, a sign that spring is on its way. Candlemas, which is the Catholic festival of the purification of the Virgin and the blessing of candles, is celebrated on February 2. The third important festival that has influenced Imbolc is Lá Fhéile Bhríd, or Brigid's Feast Day. Celebrated in Ireland and the outer isles of Britain and Scotland, this festival honors the goddess (later saint) Brigid. The original translation of her name in Irish Gaelic meant "bright flame," and from this translation the association of Brigid with fire and light arose.

Key to the concept of Imbolc are the first stirrings of the potential for life after a period of seeming lifelessness. As the weather varies so drastically among the places where people who practice alternative spirituality live, focusing on the return of spring during Imbolc can have less meaning than the concept of purification in your ritual. On the other hand, depending on your locale, perhaps the promise of coming spring is a welcome concept after you've been frozen in snow and ice for a few months!

A symbolic action derived from the old Irish Imbolc traditions is to leave a ribbon or a square of cloth outdoors overnight, where it is said that Brigid will bless it as she passes on her feast night. This cloth or ribbon can then be used to aid you in healing spells and rituals during the year.

Vernal Equinox
◊ **March 20–23: when the sun passes into the sign of Aries**

The vernal equinox is the first day of spring. Unlike the solstices, there is little evidence that pre-Christian people celebrated the equinoxes, and thus the equinox festivals tend to be even more obscure in their sources than the other sabbats.

Another name for this spring festival is Ostara, popularly thought to be derived from that of a Saxon goddess of spring, Ostre, Ostara, or Eostre. The first recorded mention of any such goddess is in Bede's C.E. 725 work, *De temporum ratione*. Other than Bede's statement, there is no evidence of the existence of such a deity in the Germanic mythos, not even in the Eddas, the main source of Germanic myth and deities.

The Saxon word *eastre* translates roughly to "beginning," and extends to the Saxon term *Estor-monath*, which means "month of beginnings" or "month of openings"—basically their term for *spring*. The English word *east* is likely derived from the same etymological root in the Germanic language group, a root associated with the concept of dawn, light, shining, and new beginnings. Other languages use the Hebrew base *peh-samech-chet* ("protection" and "compassion") to describe the festival of rebirth, fertility, and light. All these concepts are associated with the vernal equinox, when light and dark are balanced during the inexorable increase begun by the sun at the winter solstice.

In a way, the spring equinox sits in an awkward position between the two other spring-like festivals. Imbolc celebrates the returning light, the first signs of spring, and the stirring of fertility in herd animals, whereas Beltaine takes for itself the joyous celebration of fertility in land and people. The vernal equinox therefore focuses on the confirmed end of winter and the sowing of crops.

Beltaine

◊ **May 1 or April 30: or when the sun reaches 15 degrees of Taurus**

The related themes in Beltaine are fertility and the blessing of fields and newly sprouted crops. This is one of the most secularized holy days in the Wheel of the Year. In some areas of western Europe the games and traditions associated with May Day have carried on. The neo-pagan focus on this time of great fertility and growth has resurrected a general secular interest in these games and traditions in North America.

Beltaine is the third and final festival of fertility. For the ancient Celts, who recognized only two seasons (growth and suspension), it was the beginning of summer.

This festival is a celebration to honor life in all its forms, just as Samhain is the celebration to honor death as an essential part of the life cycle. And as at Samhain, it is said that the veil between the worlds is thin. This means that the otherworld, the realm of the gods, magic, and spirits, is very close to our world. At Beltaine it is less difficult to connect to the realm of the gods through ritual or meditation because of the greater harmony that exists between the energies of our world and the energies of the otherworld.

Beltaine is a time of great joy, but it is not a time simply for sexual licentiousness, as more puritanical folk through the centuries have perceived it to be. The physical sexual act is one of the methods by which we perpetuate life, but in the *grander* scheme sex symbolizes so much more than mere physical pleasure; it mirrors the act of creation.

Midsummer

◊ **June 20–23: when the sun passes into the sign of Cancer**

The summer solstice celebrates the sun at the peak of its power. Modern practitioners sometimes call this festival Litha, which comes from the Saxon word for "light." Again, as with Ostara, this is a word that seems to have been associated with a general time of year—not with a specific holy day and certainly not with a deity. Midsummer is a time of great light; the days are long and the nights are short. The crops are abundant and everywhere there is life. The Goddess, like Mother Nature herself, is carrying young, and her developing motherhood is reflected in the abundance growing in the fields. Like The Empress of the tarot's Major Arcana, she is fertility itself.

Secular Midsummer rituals in Europe usually celebrate the sun at its height of power and glory, as well as the abundance of crops growing in the fields. This festival also holds within it the simultaneous realization that from this day on, the sun loses its height and brightness slightly each day. The cycle continues; the seed of destruction lies at the heart of every triumph.

Like many of the Beltaine traditions, the traditions associated with Midsummer became quite secularized and were performed all over western and northern Europe into the twenty-first century. The central symbol associated with Midsummer is the bonfire, signifying the brightness and prevalence of the sun at its powerful peak.

Lughnassadh/Lammas

◊ **August 2: or when the sun reaches 15 degrees of Leo**

Lughnassadh is a Celtic-based festival to open the harvest season, and it is the first of the three harvest festivals. Intimately connected with the concept of corn and grain, Lughnassadh celebrates the success of the previous fertility festivals and of the life cycle as seed turns to fruit.

The sabbat is named for Lugh, a Celtic god, and some believe Lughnassadh commemorates the wake of his foster mother. There are many gatherings held at this time of year wherein trade and games of skill are featured, both of which are commonly associated with Lugh, known as the many-skilled god. The other major influence for this festival is the Anglo-Saxon celebration known as Lammas. This comes from the Anglo-Saxon *hloef-mas*, or "loaf mass," a Christian celebration of the first fruits of the field, the main offering of which is the bread made with the first gatherings of wheat and grain.

Autumn Equinox

◊ **September 20–23: when the sun passes into the sign of Libra**

Of the three sabbats associated with the harvest, the autumn equinox is the major festival of thanksgiving and plenty. It is sometimes called Mabon by many modern practitioners because of the Welsh myth of a hero traveling to the underworld to rescue Mabon, paralleling other harvest-related Indo-European myths of rescuing young people from the underworld.

At harvest, celebrate successes for the achievements they are, and reflect upon how those successes came to be. It should be remembered that harvest is still a season of activity and work. No crop is ever gathered by sitting back and congratulating oneself upon how well it has been tended. This festival balances that activity with pause to give due recognition to the effort involved in every step of the process that led to current success. Harvest embraces both the hard labor and the necessary rest that punctuates labor.

Balance is an important theme associated with this sabbat—as it is with Ostara, the vernal equinox. Again the hours of day and night keep pace; again light and dark meet as equals. From this day forward, the darkness will gain upon the light, which will continue to fade in a more noticeable fashion. Harvest marks the threshold of light and dark, the fine line between life and death. While the solstices celebrate the points where an extreme is reached, the equinoxes focus on liminal states, the moments where a precise balance moves to one side or another of a still point.

Samhain

◊ **October 31: or when the sun reaches 15 degrees of Scorpio**

Samhain is the third and final harvest festival in the Wheel of the Year. As the seasonal year is a wheel, this final sabbat is also the beginning; all ends hold within them the promise of a new birth. The ancient Celts recognized only two basic seasons—summer and winter. Just as summer began with Beltaine, Samhain signals the beginning of the winter season.

Samhain marks the time of quiet and reflection that will occupy our minds and hearts until Yule, or Midwinter, when the light will once again be reborn. Samhain marks a period of solemn introspection and evaluation, and subsequently the preparation for the fallow period, when the earth sleeps and regenerates its energy. As at Beltaine, the veil between the worlds thins. The otherworld, or spirit realm, seems much closer to us, and we are allowed to communicate with those beyond the veil. With its solemn focus on the importance of death as an essential element within the cycle of life, it is perhaps unsurprising that Samhain is also the celebration of ancestral dead, and the period of mourning for the slain god.

As in other sabbats, the spiritual celebration has been secularized, and the holiday of Halloween bears little resemblance to the spiritual themes associated with Samhain.

⟿ Colors, Deities, and Animals ⟿

Collecting information on other objects or concepts that carry energy is always an enriching activity, and makes your grimoire a repository of knowledge and information to consult when you need ideas. This section collects a variety of references that you may find useful.

Color Correspondences

These are common Western occult correspondences for color, but always defer to your own personal associations. If you loathe the color blue, for example, it's not going to make a spell to improve communication work for you; in fact, it would probably have the opposite effect. Make your own personal lists after experimenting. Your experiences are always the most valid reference you have.

◊ **Black:** dispels negative energy, absorbs negativity, repels evil, mystery, fertility, regeneration

◊ **Blue:** cleanses, purifies negativity, encourages truth and communication, spirituality, tranquility, peace, justice, healing

◊ **Brown:** transformation, earth, property, stability, home, career

◊ **Gold:** energy, success, health, prosperity, solar energy, masculine energy

◊ **Gray:** calm, spirit work, gentle closure, neutralizing energy or situations

◊ **Green:** healing, calm, property/possessions, finances, prosperity, nature

◊ **Orange:** abundance, career, acceptance, self-esteem, motivation, success, speed, action

◊ **Pink:** affection, friendship

◊ **Purple:** occult power, spirituality

◊ **Red:** power, energy, stopping or removing something, life, passion, action

◊ **Silver:** purity, divination, psychic work, feminine energy, spirit, lunar energy

◊ **Violet:** mysticism, meditation, spirituality

◊ **White:** purifies, soothes, represents wholeness and new beginnings, psychic development

◊ **Yellow:** happiness and joy, clarity, communication, safe travels, happy home, intellectual matters

Deities

Learning about new deities and their areas of sovereignty in their respective cultures is enriching, and offers you insight into how godforms and various manifestations of the divine express themselves. If you already honor a deity (or deities), learning as much as you can about them will inform your practice. If you are seeking a deity to pledge your service to, reading broadly will help you. Look up preferred offerings, kinds of worship, associated myths, and the culture they come from to get a well-rounded sense of these beings.

◊ **Anubis (Egyptian):** God of judgment, passage to the underworld, lost souls, orphans. Associated symbols are the flail, crook, and scepter.

◊ **Aphrodite (Greek):** Goddess of love, beauty, fertility. Roman cognate Venus. Associated animal is the dove.

◊ **Apollo (Greek/Roman):** God of poetry and the arts, divination, protection, sun, healing. Associated symbols are arrows and the lyre.

◊ **Ares (Greek):** God of war, battle, courage. Roman cognate Mars. Associated animal is the dog.

◊ **Artemis (Greek):** Goddess of unmarried women, childbirth, women's mysteries, hunting, the moon. Roman cognate Diana. Associated animals are hounds and deer.

◊ **Athena (Greek):** Goddess of wisdom, defensive war, Athens. Roman cognate Minerva. Associated animal is the owl.

◊ **Baldur (Norse):** God of beauty, love, purity, peace, righteousness. Associated symbol is mistletoe.

◊ **Brigid (Celtic):** Goddess of creativity, fire, inspiration, healing, hearth and home. Associated symbol is Brigid's cross woven of reeds or straw.

◊ **Cerridwen (Celtic):** Goddess of transformation, cauldron of inspiration, wisdom, prophecy. Associated animal is the sow.

◊ **Dagda (Celtic):** Father god, fertility, knowledge, abundance. Associated symbols are the staff and cauldron.

◊ **Demeter (Greek):** Goddess of the harvest, nature. Roman cognate Ceres. Associated symbol is the sheaf of wheat.

◊ **Dionysus (Greek):** God of wine, theater. Associated symbol is the wine cup.

◊ **Epona (Celtic):** Goddess of fertility, agriculture, horses. Associated symbols are the platter and ears of wheat.

◊ **Freyja (Norse):** Goddess of abundance, battle, wealth, magic, prophecy. Sister of Freyr. Associated animals are cats and falcons.

◊ **Freyr (Norse):** God of agriculture, prosperity, life, fertility. Brother of Freyja. Associated animal is the boar.

◊ **Frigg (Norse):** Goddess of household management, family relationships, marriage, prophecy. Associated symbol is the spinning wheel.

◊ **Hades (Greek):** God of the underworld. Roman cognate Pluto. Associated animal is the three-headed dog Cerberus.

◊ **Hathor (Egyptian):** Goddess of love, music, joy, dance, song, mothers, children. Associated animal is the cow.

◊ **Hekate (Greek):** Goddess of magic, the spirit world, liminal stages, rites of passage. Associated symbols are keys, torches, and crossroads.

◊ **Hera (Greek):** Goddess of marriage, women. Roman cognate Juno. Associated animal is the peacock.

◊ **Hermes (Greek):** Messenger god and god of luck, thievery, travel. Roman cognate Mercury. Associated symbol is the caduceus.

◊ **Hestia (Greek):** Goddess of the hearth. Roman cognate Vesta. Associated symbol is the hearth fire.

◊ **Holda (Germanic):** Goddess of winter, weather, textiles, fertility, childbirth. Associated animals are the stork, goose, and swan.

◊ **Horus (Egyptian):** God of kingship, pharaonic power, the sky; represents the living pharaoh. Associated symbols are the falcon and the Eye of Horus.

◊ **Isis (Egyptian):** Mother goddess, protection, healing. Associated animals are the cow and falcon.

◊ **Lugh (Celtic):** God of all skills, prophecy, marksmanship, healing, arts and crafts.

◊ **Ma'at (Egyptian):** Goddess of truth, order. Associated symbols are the scales and white feather.

◊ **Manannan Mac Lir (Celtic):** God of the sea, the otherworld. Associated symbol is the boat.

◊ **Morrigan (Celtic):** Goddess of sovereignty, battle. Associated animal is the raven.

◊ **Odin (Norse):** The Allfather, god of wisdom, secrets, sacrifice. Associated animals are wolves and ravens.

◊ **Osiris (Egyptian):** God of fertility, agriculture, death and rebirth, afterlife; represents the dead pharaoh. Associated symbols are the crook and flail.

◊ **Persephone (Greek):** Goddess of spring, growth. Roman cognate Proserpina. Associated symbol is the pomegranate.

◊ **Poseidon (Greek):** God of the sea, horses. Roman cognate Neptune. Associated symbol is the trident.

◊ **Rhiannon (Celtic):** Goddess of sovereignty, travel, the otherworld. Associated animals are the horse and bird.

◊ **Thor (Norse):** God of storms, warriors, strength, protection, war, thunder and lightning. Associated symbol is the hammer.

◊ **Thoth (Egyptian):** God of writing, knowledge. Associated animal is the ibis.

◊ **Tyr (Norse):** God of war, justice in battle, victory, heroic glory. Associated symbol is the spear.

◊ **Zeus (Greek):** God of sky, thunder. Roman cognate Jupiter. Associated symbol is the lightning bolt. Associated animal is the eagle.

Animals

Being able to call on the energies of animals to support or lend energy to your work is a skill that many witches practice. Studying an animal and asking it to teach you its wisdom is a serious undertaking, one that requires commitment, but that is enriching and yields great knowledge.

To start your section on animal correspondences, here are a few animals commonly encountered in magical practice.

◊ **Bear:** Sovereignty, power, strength, guardian

◊ **Blue jay:** Intelligence, risk taking, seizing opportunity, boldness, curiosity, family bonds

◊ **Butterfly:** Transformation, grace, joy, lightness, cycles of growth, rebirth

◊ **Crow:** Luck, tricksters, deceit, magic, fearlessness, adaptability

◊ **Deer:** Compassion, peace, intellectual, caring, kind, gentleness

◊ **Dog:** Protection, loyalty, trustworthiness, perseverance

◊ **Dove:** Hope, love, faith, calm, peace

◊ **Dragonfly:** Adaptability, change, new life, seeing through illusion

◊ **Falcon:** New beginnings, leadership, insight, guardianship, superiority

◊ **Fox:** Cunning, agility, quick-witted, diplomacy, invisibility

◊ **Horse:** Power, stamina, freedom, travel, nobility

◊ **Owl:** Wisdom, intuition, insight, mystery, secrets, stealth

◊ **Rabbit:** Caution, fertility, creativity, feminine energy, luck, abundance

◊ **Raven:** Magic, revelation, healing, introspection, secrets

◊ **Robin:** New beginnings, change, hope, happiness

◊ **Snake:** Healing, primal energy, transformation, renewal

◊ **Spider:** Creativity, patience, control over your path, shadow self

◊ **Swan:** Dreams, intuition, serenity, balance of different areas of life, beauty, love

◊ **Tiger:** Willpower, trusting the self, unpredictability, personal power, vitality

◊ **Wolf:** Teaching, discipline, loyalty, perseverance, protection, intuition

Common Magical Tools

A section on magical tools and their associations is not uncommon in a grimoire. As you advance, collecting interesting facts about different cultural expressions of these kinds of tools can inform your practice and challenge you to look at things differently. Remember, your grimoire itself is also a magical tool, containing knowledge and energy.

The Knife/Athame

The knife is a symbol of air or fire, depending on which Western occult tradition you subscribe to, and in some paths the knife is commonly used in a symbolic fashion. The partner to this tool is the boline, a knife used for actual physical cutting and slicing in a ritual context for things such as herbs, wood, and so forth. The boline sometimes has a white handle or a curved blade, while the knife is generally dark-handled and has a straight blade with two edges. Sometimes the knife is sharpened; sometimes it is left dull to demonstrate that it is a metaphysical tool. If you're a practical witch who uses everyday tools for magical purposes as well, it makes more sense to recognize the spiritual associations of the knives you already use. Knives are generally associated with action, decisiveness, resolve, and confidence.

The Wand

Another traditional tool is the wand. The wand is a symbol of either fire or air (depending on what your belief concerning the knife is, the wand is assigned to the other). Fairy tales feature fairies and sorceresses with magical wands that transform and enchant; tales of wizards and druids often feature staves. Both the wand and the staff are symbolic of the same thing. Staves tend to be associated with solidity and grounding as well, reflecting the world tree and the axis mundi found in shamanic societies. The obvious modern tool that parallels the wand is the wooden spoon, a tool of transformation and blending.

The Broom

Another ubiquitous magical symbol is the broom. Like the staff, it symbolizes grounding, but it also symbolizes the spiritual flights taken seeking knowledge from other spirits and worlds. The broom is said to be a union of the female and male symbols of brush and staff, and as such was used in fertility ceremonies, festivals, and rituals, especially to encourage crops to grow. In more modern magical use, it is used to sweep the energy of a place clean of negativity. In this capacity it is sometimes termed a besom and is often kept apart from the everyday broom used to sweep up crumbs and dirt off the floor. If you use your everyday tools for magical purposes because every act is a spiritual act, using the everyday broom means the floor and the energy get swept clean together.

The Cup

The cup is variously used to hold the physical representation of water on the altar, as a receptacle or an offering, or as a vessel to share communion. A thrifty witch or someone who has limited space can use it for all three. You can pour out the water you bless as a representation of elemental energy, as an offering to trees or plants outdoors, or give it to your houseplants; you may even drink the water you bless. Taking it into your body during the ritual is a wonderful way to absorb the qualities of the element of water. (Do this only if you haven't added anything to it during the blessing process, and only if whatever tool you may have touched to it during the consecration or blessing is clean.)

A simple cup (ceramic is ideal) is a useful item. Water is one of the four physical (and metaphysical) elements, and witches often like to have a representation of each element nearby as they work. A cup reserved exclusively to hold water in this way honors the element of water. In addition, the cup is useful to drink from in a ritual setting. Some witches use any cup from the cupboard they feel like using at the time, because it's what's in the cup that counts.

The Pentacle

The pentacle comes from the ceremonial magic elements and isn't original to witchcraft, but has made its way there during the twentieth century. The pentacle is a flat disk of wood, earthenware, or metal, inscribed with the five-pointed star known as the pentagram. The points of the star may reach the edges of the disk or may stop about an inch from the edge, and an engraved circle may surround the star. The pentacle represents the element of earth or spirit on your altar. It's not only symbolic, however. It can be used to ground objects or to charge them. You can place food offerings on it. While the pentagram is a common symbol on the pentacle, you can experiment with other symbols, such as triskeles, ankhs, Celtic knots, and other meaningful symbols that inform your practice and personal spirituality.

The Altar

The altar is a basic workspace. It's not necessarily a permanent fixture, especially in the case of a witch who lives with non-witches, or one who lives in limited space. For some witches, any workspace is a magical workspace. Others like a formal space dedicated to it, whether it's permanent or set up anew each time.

Wherever you set up your altar, make sure you leave enough room to move around it. An ideal position for the altar is right in the center of your circle or sacred space, which allows you the freedom of movement to access it from any angle.

If you are lucky enough to have a permanent altar, you may have to leave it where it is and build your circles around it. A permanent altar can literally store energy for you. Rather than grounding excess energy into the earth or into your tools at the end of a ritual, ground it into the altar. As a focus for worship, your altar builds in energy as you practice; using this method of grounding means that your altar eventually develops into a tool with power of its own that you can tap in to.

Stones and Crystals

Sometimes called the bones of the earth, stones are a reusable resource in witchcraft. They are easily cleansed of previous energy and programmed purpose, and re-empowered for a new goal. Stones are easy to carry in a pocket or in a larger bag, can be worn as jewelry, and can be arranged in bowls or on shelves. This section has notes to help you start your own reference for stones and crystals.

Agate (Moss)

Moss agate is used for healing, for calm, and for stress relief. Moss agate looks like strands of moss caught in ice or in a translucent, blurry crystal. Like most green stones, it is associated with nature.

Amethyst

Amethyst is purple quartz and is associated with psychic power, truth, balance, protection, and healing.

Aventurine

Aventurine is a green opaque stone with tiny flecks of gold in it. It is associated with luck, prosperity, and health.

Bloodstone

Bloodstone is a green opaque stone with flecks of red in it. Magically, it is associated with health (especially of the blood) and protection.

Citrine

Citrine is yellow quartz and often appears as yellow ice or is yellow and white. It is found in points and as a tumbled stone. It works to calm nightmares, aids in digestion, focuses the mind, and enhances creativity.

Hematite

Hematite is a dull silver-colored stone (it can also show up as black, brown, and reddish-brown). In the Middle Ages, it was called a bloodstone, so if you come across a reference to a bloodstone make sure you know which stone is being referred to. Hematite has iron in it and magically is associated with grounding excess or unbalanced energy. It also deflects negativity and is thus associated with defense, healing, and justice.

Jasper

Found in many colors, jasper is most commonly red. It is good for grounding and stabilizing energy and for protection and courage. Bury jaspers in the four corners of your garden to deepen its connection to the earth and secure its energy for more balanced growth and yield.

Lapis Lazuli

A deep blue stone with flecks of gold, lapis lazuli is associated with leadership, communication, stress relief, creativity, joy, and harmony.

Malachite

A deep green stone with bands or circles of lighter green, malachite is associated with fertility and earth mysteries. Malachite is a wonderful stone for green witches to work with, for it helps strengthen your connection to the world of nature. Try carrying or wearing a piece of malachite while you communicate with the world of green, whether you are tramping through a field or digging in your backyard. See how it affects your work and your perceptions.

Moonstone

A milky-white stone, sometimes with overtones of green, peach, or gray, the moonstone is magically associated with children, love, peace, and protection during travel. It also has a connection to the Goddess.

Quartz (Clear)

An easily obtained stone, a clear quartz crystal looks like ice, often with small inclusions (which do not affect the stone's energy at all). Quartz crystal amplifies energy, stores power, enhances psychic ability, and absorbs negativity. It has become immensely popular and can be found in tumbled form and in point form (which is how it grows) and is often set in jewelry. Quartz crystal is an excellent all-purpose stone to work with.

Quartz (Rose)

Another common stone, rose quartz looks like pink ice. Like other quartz crystals, rose quartz amplifies and stores energy. Rose quartz is specifically used to boost self-esteem and encourage self-love, for emotional healing, to foster affection, and to transform negative energy into positive, supportive energy.

Sodalite

A dark blue stone with white or gray veins, sodalite is used for balancing emotions and enhancing wisdom.

Tiger's Eye

A glossy, satiny brown stone with bands of dark gold, the tiger's eye is used for strength, courage, luck, and prosperity.

Turquoise

A pale blue stone with fine black or gray lines running through it, turquoise is an excellent children's stone, for it protects and strengthens gently. It also helps focus the mind and will.

✦Herb and Plant Correspondences✦

Working with the energies of nature is one of the joys of witchcraft, and one of the easiest ways to do that is with plants. Many you can find in the spice section of a grocery store, or outside through wildcrafting. Generally, a plant referred to as an herb possesses some sort of medicinal, culinary, or magical value, and they make up a large part of a witch's practice.

The following list of herbs covers very common examples that you may already have in your pantry or are easily found fresh.

Allspice
(Pimenta officinalis)

Also known as pimento or Jamaica pepper, the allspice berry is picked from an evergreen tree in the myrtle family. When the berry is dried (its most common form) it resembles a large peppercorn. Called "allspice" because it incorporates flavors such as clove, cinnamon, and nutmeg, it is a common flavoring for spice cookies and many stews and meat dishes. Magically, allspice is said to draw business success and money to a person. Allspice berries also make wonderful additions to prosperity blends and magic that focuses on increasing energy, love, healing, and luck.

Basil
(Ocimum basilicum)

Also known as sweet basil and St. Joseph's wort, basil is used in cuisines worldwide. Basil is technically a member of the mint family and its leaves are used both fresh and dried to flavor meats, salads, and sauces. Medicinally, basil offers antibacterial properties and can even pro-tect your cells from sun damage. Magically, basil is excellent for many purposes, but especially for love magic. Basil is used for love, protection, prosperity, success, peace, happiness, purification, and tranquility.

Bay
(Laurus nobilis)

Bay (or bay laurel) is an aromatic leaf that is commonly used in cooking in whole, dried, and ground forms. While some forms of laurel are poisonous, bay leaves are not despite the oft-repeated belief that they are. Bay is a popular element in aromatherapy and in several herbal treatments for skin and respiratory conditions. Bay can help with digestive problems as well as help reduce anxiety and stress. Magically, bay is associated with success, wisdom, and divination. If you are looking for guidance on a particular goal, write your wish on a bay leaf and sleep with it under your pillow for dreams that will show you how to pursue your goal.

Chamomile
(Chamaemelum nobile, Matricaria recutita)

Also known as manzanilla, chamomile is considered one of the most ancient and versatile medicinal herbs. Both the Roman and German varieties of the plant are popular as magical and medicinal herbs. Chamomile is excellent for soothing stomach problems, headaches, and anxiety and is gentle enough to be given to children. Magically, it is used for prosperity, peace, healing, harmony, and happiness.

Cinnamon
(Cinnamomum spp.)

Cinnamon is one of the must-have multipurpose herbs in a witch's stock. Cinnamon is derived from the inner bark of several tree species and boasts a wide variety of health benefits for the body including antibacterial, antifungal, and antidiabetic properties. It possesses a great amount of energy, and a pinch can be added to any spell to boost the power. Cinnamon is also useful in spells that involve money. Magically, cinnamon is associated with success, action, healing, protection, energy, love, prosperity, and purification.

Clove
(Syzygium aromaticum)

The small dried flower bud of the clove plant is used in cooking, baking, and magic. In cooking, cloves have a warm, sweet, and identifiable flavor. They are often used in Indian and Middle Eastern dishes but also can be found studding baked hams and as an ingredient in pumpkin spice and Chinese five-spice mixes. Magically, clove is associated with protection, purification, mental ability, and healing. Try adding three cloves to a sachet or charm to tie in protective and purifying energy. A sachet of rosemary, angelica, sage, three cloves, and a pinch of salt tied shut with red thread or ribbon is good to hang above a door to turn away negativity and protect the area.

Ginger
(Zingiber officinale)

Ginger is a powerful anti-inflammatory herb and has been used medicinally as a remedy for nausea and indigestion, colds and flus, poor circulation, menstrual cramps, arthritis, headaches, and joint problems, among others. Ginger is also used in a variety of foods, including candy, soda, pickles, and alcoholic beverages. Magically, ginger root is ideal to add to rituals and spells because it acts like a booster for the power involved. Its warming heat revs up the energy associated with your work. Ginger can also be used to jump-start love, stimulate finances, and increase the potential for success.

Mint
(Mentha spp.)

There is a wide variety of green or garden mints, which are hardy and easy to grow in a garden or on your kitchen windowsill. Be warned, however, that left to its devices mint will spread quickly and become a nuisance in your garden. The impressive list of health benefits for mint includes improved digestion, breath freshening, and relief from nausea, depression, fatigue, and headaches. It can also be used topically for certain skin problems. Make an infusion to help with headaches, stimulating the appetite, and aiding digestion. Magical associations are prosperity, joy, fertility, purification, love, and success.

Mugwort
(Artemisia vulgaris)

Mugwort has been used since ancient times to battle fatigue and as a protection against evil spirits and wild animals. The plant contains a number of antioxidants that have been shown to alleviate digestive and intestinal issues like ulcers, vomiting, and constipation. It is also known to elicit intense and vivid dreams. Try using a decoction of the leaves before divination to help open your mind. Magically, mugwort is associated with prophetic dreams, relaxation and tranquility, protection, banishing, and consecration.

Parsley
(Petroselinum crispum)

In ancient Greece, parsley was so sacred that they used it to adorn the victors of their athletic contests and as a way to decorate the tombs of the dead. Parsley is commonly used as a culinary herb and is high in iron, vitamin C, and vitamin K. Both the seeds and the leaves can be used in cooking and in your magical applications. Magically, parsley is associated with power, strength, lust, purification, and prosperity.

Rosemary
(Rosmarinus officinalis)

Rosemary is a woody herb with evergreen needles and white, pink, purple, or blue flowers. In ancient times, mourners would often throw it into graves as a remembrance for the dead. Nowadays, you can plant it by your front door for protection, make an essential oil out of it that can be used for cleansing, and of course include it in your cooking. An infusion taken as a tea will help ease a headache. Magical associations include protection, improving memory, wisdom, health, and healing.

Sage
(Salvia spp.)

Sage belongs to the mint family along with other herbs such as oregano, rosemary, and thyme. Sage adds an earthy flavor to foods and is loaded with antioxidants. In magic it is commonly used for purification and protection, and for banishing negative energy. An infusion taken as a tea will help settle a sour stomach, ease digestion, and calm anxiety as well. In addition to purification and protection, magical associations include wisdom, health, and long life.

Verbena
(Verbena officinalis, Verbena spp.)

Also known as vervain and enchanter's herb, verbena is a perennial herb native to Europe. It grows tall and straight with toothed leaves and spikes that hold clusters of flowers. Medicinally, verbena is used for sore throats, respiratory diseases, digestive disorders, and even stress and anxiety. Magically versatile, verbena is associated with divination, protection, inspiration, abundance, love, peace, tranquility, healing, prosperity, skill in artistic performance, and the reversal of negative activity. You can make a verbena oil by infusing the fresh plant in a light olive oil or grapeseed oil and then use it as a standard blessing oil. It is also an excellent herb to add to any charm bag or spell to encourage success.

Yarrow
(Achillea millefolium)

Yarrow is a member of the sunflower family and is a common North American plant that is easy to care for. Yarrow has large flower heads composed of many tiny, tightly packed daisy-like flowers usually in white or lavender. The herb can be taken internally to treat colds, fevers, and indigestion, and it can also be used topically in skin treatments. Magically, yarrow is used for courage, healing, and love.

Recording Information

When you gather information about herbs and other plants, there is a wealth of detail you can include. The previous notes are brief beginnings that you can expand upon. Following is a list of the kind of information you might choose to record in your grimoire:

◊ Name of the plant

◊ Physical description and traits

◊ Illustration

◊ Toxicity/warnings

◊ Geographic information

◊ Medical information

◊ Practical and historical uses

◊ Traditional magical information

◊ Your personal magical information/ experiences

◊ Samples of the plant

Stress Relief Tincture

Herbs and plants can be used in many ways in your spiritual and magical practice. This tincture, which can help alleviate the effects of stress on your body and mind, is just one example. Experiment to discover what works for you, and keep track of the results in your grimoire.

A tincture is an alcohol-based herbal extract, made by macerating plant matter in alcohol. As a rule, dried herbs need more liquid (a 1:5 ratio of dried plant matter to alcohol) than fresh (roughly 1:3 herbs to alcohol), and thicker, woodier plant matter will need more time to macerate.

If alcohol is contraindicated for you or you are sensitive to it, this can be made with vinegar instead of vodka. The extract will not be as strong, nor will it keep as long as alcohol-based tinctures; six months is the extent of a vinegar-based tincture's shelf life, as after that the properties of the herbs begin to deteriorate. An alcohol-based tincture will keep for approximately a year in a cool, dark place.

This tincture calls for lemon balm and valerian, two herbs that are commonly used for relaxation. They are not in the previous reference section on herbs. Before you make this tincture, research both herbs and write down the botanical names as well as medicinal, magical, and practical uses for them in the second part of this book.

What You Need:
- ¼ cup fresh lemon balm
- ¼ cup fresh valerian
- Jar with a lid (at least 12 ounces)
- 1 cup vodka
- Fine sieve or cheesecloth
- 8-ounce bottle with cap

What to Do:
1. Chop the plant matter and place it in the jar. Muddle it to bruise the leaves further and expose as many surfaces as possible.
2. Pour the vodka over the plant matter and stir. Close the jar.
3. Leave the jar in a cool, dark place to steep. Swirl or gently shake it every day or two.
4. Taste the tincture after two weeks; if you can taste the plant flavor in the alcohol, that's a good sign. You can strain the mixture through a sieve or cheesecloth and pour it into the bottle, or leave it another week to get stronger.
5. Store in a cool, dark place.

How to Use:

Take ¹/₃ teaspoon an hour before bedtime. (Usually the tincture is mixed with a glass of water or a cup of hot water to be sipped like tea. The flavor can be strong, so diluting it makes it easier to take. The alcohol flavor burns off when mixed into freshly boiled water, so that can be a plus for people too.)

> Commercial tinctures are usually sold in small bottles with eyedroppers, and dosage is measured by number of drops. Generally, a drop from an eyedropper is 0.05 ml. Thirty drops would be 1.5 ml, or about ¹/₃ teaspoon. That's really not a lot of tincture, but don't be tempted to up the dose. Tinctures are stronger than teas.

Divination

Divination is a form of communicating with energy and knowledge that is ordinarily more difficult to access. Often a tool is used to facilitate this. This section gives a brief overview of some of the most common divination tools.

Tarot

Tarot decks are one of the most familiar divination tools. Beautiful inspirational art paired with traditional symbology appeals to many people. A tarot deck has seventy-eight cards: twenty-two Major Arcana and fifty-six Minor Arcana.

> Tarot cards are similar to other systems referenced in magical work in that associations may vary among specific tools; for example, the association of Swords and Wands flips depending on the tarot deck you use. Find a deck that matches your personal association of elements with the tools, otherwise the symbolism depicted in the art might cause conflict for you. Likewise, some decks have different numbering for the Major Arcana cards, notably flipping the position of Strength and Justice; this will probably have less of an impact on you than the Minor Arcana symbolism.

The twenty-two Major Arcana cards represent life's deep spiritual lessons. They portray the stages of a journey to spiritual self-awareness. Each Major Arcana card features a figure or a scene representing a specific energy. The number of the card, the name, and keywords for the themes they address are as follows:

◊ **0 The Fool:** new beginnings, innocence, surprise

◊ **I The Magician:** confidence, mastery, application of will

◊ **II The High Priestess:** intuition, secrets, mysteries

◊ **III The Empress:** fertility, fruition, fulfillment

◊ **IV The Emperor:** leadership, authority

◊ **V The Hierophant:** tradition, conservatism, conformity

◊ **VI The Lovers:** choice between two outcomes, harmony, love (romantic or otherwise)

◊ **VII The Chariot:** travel, self-discipline, overcoming obstacles

◊ **VIII Strength:** courage, endurance, gentle control

◊ **IX The Hermit:** wisdom, contemplation

◊ **X Wheel of Fortune:** karma, destiny, change of fortune

◊ **XI Justice:** balance, legal matters, impartiality

◊ **XII The Hanged Man:** change of approach, different worldview, self-sacrifice

◊ **XIII Death:** end to a major situation, change

◊ **XIV Temperance:** patience, renewal, emotional balance

◊ **XV The Devil:** obsession, addiction, manipulation

◊ **XVI The Tower:** upheaval, major changes

◊ **XVII The Star:** optimism, healing

◊ **XVIII The Moon:** uncertainty, illusion

◊ **XIX The Sun:** success, happiness

◊ **XX Judgment:** reaping what was sown, consequences of past choices

◊ **XXI The World:** triumph, resolution

The fifty-six Minor Arcana cards reflect the challenges encountered on a daily basis. They address more practical issues, and may pertain to temporary situations or minor influences. The Minor Arcana is divided into four suits: Pentacles (or Coins), Swords, Wands (or Rods), and Cups. Each suit has a different element and theme(s) associated with it.

◊ **Pentacles:** Earth; finance, material issues

◊ **Swords:** Air; intellect, clarity

◊ **Wands:** Fire; action, business, activity

◊ **Cups:** Water; emotions, relationships

The cards all have reversed meanings as well, if a card shows up upside-down. You can take this to mean the reverse of the card's meaning, or that you should pay specific attention to the card.

Pendulum

The pendulum is another divination tool; intuitive witches, especially those on the green path, often favor this tool. Albert Einstein, who had an interest in dowsing, once said, "The dowsing rod is a simple instrument which shows the reaction of the human nervous system to certain factors which are unknown to us at this time." Like the dowsing rod, the pendulum is an object that responds to minuscule movements initiated by the nervous system, prompted by the body reacting to messages coming from the energy around it. Pendulums can be made from crystals, wood, or metals, and can be as simple as any sort of weight hanging from a string.

Scrying

Anther intuitive divination method is scrying, in which you use an item as a visual focus to allow your mind to disconnect from the physical world and be open to images, ideas, and visions. This device is referred to as a speculum. For example, the archetypical crystal ball is a scrying tool; black mirrors are also popular; bowls of water or ink, polished stones, and even candle flames are all used as a visual focus in order to shift consciousness to receive impressions regarding a problem or situation. These tools serve as a visual focus to occupy the conscious mind while the subconscious mind becomes active. A relaxed, dreamy state enables us to perceive more than we do when we think we are alert and conscious of our environment. When we are "alert" in this way, we are in fact focusing a little too hard on the world around us. When relaxed, we are more likely to trust our intuition, which is what divination is all about.

How to Record a Divination

Recording divinations can be tricky. Some people believe that the entire layout of cards or tiles should be noted down, while others think that just jotting down your general impression of each divination is adequate.

Here is the sort of information that diviners find useful to record:

◊   The date and time

◊   Moon phase (and sign if you know it), and any other pertinent astrological information

◊   The location of the reading

◊   The weather

◊   Your health

◊   Who is the divination for?

◊   What is the guidance for? Is there a specific question asked?

◊   System of divination used (with specific details)
   • Layout, draw, or spread used
   • Symbols in key positions (What cards, runes, or patterns emerged as important?)
   • Your initial interpretation of the spread
   • What is the overall answer to the question asked?

◊   Details you wish to remember

◊   Feedback (this allows you to note down any response you receive from the querent, both at the time of the reading and at a later date)

◊   Interpretation after research/reflection

◊   Research notes associated with symbols

◊   Later notes

If you are doing divination for yourself, then you can be as detailed as you like. You can sketch out the entire spread and indicate what symbols appeared in which positions. If you are recording information about a reading for someone else, your notes may be less detailed.

If it makes things quicker, you can snap a photo of your card spread or layout and either print it out to attach to your record later, or refer to it to write down specifics.

Spells

Designing your own spells is one of the most enjoyable parts of being a witch. You can tailor your work to your goal in many different ways, including varying the supplies and correspondences you choose, the format you employ, and the processes you use. Spells are a wonderful way to express your creativity.

The Basic Steps of a Spell

A spell is designed to initiate change on some level by shifting the balance of energy within a situation. The shift doesn't simply occur in response to your wish for a change; there are certain stages through which you must pass. Every spell is different, but most include several general steps; let's take a look at them.

1. **Establish your need or desire.** There's no point in doing a spell for the sake of doing a spell. That's simply a waste of time and energy.
2. **Compose your spell.** Take the time to think about your desired outcome and what energies you wish to harness to achieve this outcome.
3. **Shift consciousness.** In order to maximize your spellwork, you should ideally be in a spellcasting frame of mind. Our everyday, scattered, and busy brains aren't very efficient at gathering energies, melding them into a spell, and releasing them toward a goal. Shifting consciousness allows you to attain a different state of mind, filtering out the surface noise and distractions in order to concentrate and focus on what you're doing.
4. **Raise energy and release it toward your goal.** Spells are powered by the energies held by the components or ingredients you choose to use (such as herbs and stones) and by your own personal energy as well.
5. **Manifestation.** Ideally, the final step is the achievement of your goal.

Creating your own spells is an interesting and enjoyable exercise. They can be simple or quite elaborate. I'm a fan of simple, so these basic spells to start you off are straightforward.

Love Spell

This spell is designed to affirm that you are open to love coming into your life. It's not a spell to draw someone to you, nor is it something to influence someone specific.

What You Need:
- 6 rose quartz stones
- Pink candle (red or white can be used as well)
- Candleholder
- Rose petals (dried or fresh)
- Matches or lighter
- Small charm bag

What to Do:
1. Place a rose quartz just above the center of your workspace. Slightly above and to each side, set two more rose quartzes. Slightly below the first stone, place two more rose quartzes to either side, closer to the imaginary center line bisecting your first stone. Place the last stone on that center line, below the last pair of stones. If you use your imagination to connect those stones, the shape will resemble a heart.

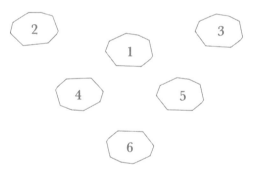

2. Place the candle and candleholder in the center of the heart, roughly between the fourth and fifth stones.
3. Sprinkle the rose petals around the whole setup.
4. Light the candle and say:

   I send my call out into the world.
   I accept love.
   I welcome it in my life.

5. Let the candle burn down. When it is finished, gather the stones and rose petals and put them in a small charm bag. Carry the bag with you.

Protection Spell

This spell is designed to protect you from illness. It's important to phrase your spell positively, so when you work, think of it as staying healthy.

What You Need:

- 1 teaspoon dried lemon peel or zest
- Malachite stone
- Clear quartz crystal
- 1 teaspoon dried lavender flowers
- Small bowl
- Small white bag (approximately 2" × 3")

What to Do:

1. Empower your supplies to defend health.
2. Place the lemon peel, malachite, quartz, and lavender in the bowl. Place the bowl on a sunny windowsill or somewhere where direct sunlight will hit it. Outdoors in unfiltered sunlight is ideal, if possible.
3. As you place the bowl, say:

   Bright sun,
   Fill these herbs and stones with your healing light.
   May they guard me from that which would disturb my wellness,
   Preserve me, and defend my health.

4. Leave the bowl in sunlight for three hours.
5. Take the components and place them inside the small bag. Tie it shut, and carry it with you.

How to Record a Spell

Here is the type of information that is good to keep track of when writing and casting spells:

1. Plan the Spell

Object/goal/purpose:

Keywords:

Ideas:

Supplies/symbols to use:

Tools:

Central symbolic action:

2. Write Out the Spell

Include statement of intent:

3. Perform the Spell

4. Record the Spell

Date/time/place:

_____

_____

Additional desired information (weather, moon phase/sign, and so on):

_____

_____

Immediate report (how it felt, how it went, and so on):

_____

_____

Any changes:

_____

_____

5. Add Notes Regarding Changes or Future Ideas

_____

_____

_____

_____

_____

6. Leave Space for Notes When Reviewing the Spell

_____

_____

_____

_____

_____

Rituals

Rituals are celebrations, an opportunity to commemorate something, or time to worship. Planning a ritual is remarkably like planning a spell (see the previous section).

Rituals usually have an opening, a central action, and a closing. Depending on how formal you want your ritual to be, the opening can include purification of the space and/or participants, a circle cast or creation of sacred space, invocation of the elements and/or quarters, and invocation of deity/deities. The closing would reverse or release all the actions you took during the opening, in reverse order: thanks given to deity/deities, thanks given to elements and/or quarters, and dismissal of circle. This section features an example of a ritual with all these different pieces of the ritual structure. After it, there is a list of suggested information to keep for each ritual you create and perform.

New Moon Ritual

This ritual is designed to mark the turning of the moon cycle, honoring the moment of shifting from the dark moon to the new moon.

What You Need:
- Matches or lighter
- Incense and censer
- Candle in candleholder (tea light or votive recommended)
- Cup of water
- Bowl of salt (or a quartz crystal)

What to Do:
1. Cast your circle or create sacred space in your preferred manner.
2. Invoke the elements to be present to witness your ritual:

- Light the incense, saying:

    Element of air, I invite you to witness this ritual.
    Bless this space with clear thought and wisdom.
    Welcome, Air.

- Light the candle, saying:

    Element of fire, I invite you to witness this ritual.
    Bless this space with creativity and action.
    Welcome, Fire.

- Hold the cup in your hands, saying:

> *Element of water, I invite you to witness this ritual.*
> *Bless this space with purity and glad spirits.*
> *Welcome, Water.*

- Hold the bowl of salt in your hands, saying:

> *Element of earth, I invite you to witness this ritual.*
> *Bless this space with stability and peace.*
> *Welcome, Earth.*

3. If you wish both the God and Goddess to be present, use this invocation as is. If you prefer only the Goddess to be present, simply leave out the references to the Lord. Hold your hands up and say:

> *Lord and Lady, I invite you to witness this ritual,*
> *As I honor the end of the lunar cycle, which is also the beginning.*
> *Bless me with your presence.*
> *Welcome, Lord and Lady.*

4. Begin your central action, which is a spoken honoring. Stand, sit, or kneel, whichever way you are comfortable. Say:

> *Dark is the night as we reach this turning point.*
> *Here is a time of death; yet a time of birth.*
> *Endings and beginnings*
> *Ebbing and flowing*
> *A journey done; a journey yet to start.*
> *We honor now the Crone-Mother;*
> *We give of our strength and in return see rebirth.*
> *Let us take a moment to think upon the things which are ending, and then upon the things which are beginning in our lives.*
> *Lady of Darkness, Grandmother, old yet ever young; we honor you as you lift your veil and show us the Maiden.*
> *Lady of new light, warrior, guide, strength and hope; we honor you who shows us the starting point, the newness of life, the fresh beginning.*
> *We honor all your faces, now and always.*
> *As the wheel turns we see birth, death, and rebirth.*
> *We know from this that every ending is a beginning; every stop a fresh starting point.*

Maiden, Mother, Crone…you are all of these and more.
Whenever we have need of anything, we can call upon you and upon this miracle of cycles,
of death and rebirth, of endings and beginnings, for you and all these abide within us.
You are She who is at the beginning and the ending of all time.
We are grateful for your love and wisdom.
Blessed Be.

5. You may stay in meditation for as long as desired at this point, or move on to thank and release those you have invited to witness. If you have not invited the God to be present to witness, simply omit the references as you say the following:

Lord and Lady, thank you for witnessing this ritual.
I am grateful for your many blessings.
You may stay or leave, as you desire.
Earth, Water, Fire, Air,
Thank you for witnessing this ritual.
I am grateful for your many blessings.
I release you.

6. Put out the candle and the incense if it is still burning. Alternatively, you may allow both to burn out on their own.

How to Record a Ritual

Record keeping for your rituals is similar to that for divination and spells. You might want to keep track of the following pertinent data related to the performance of a ritual:

1. Plan the Ritual

Object/goal/purpose:

Keywords:

Ideas:

Supplies/symbols to use:

Tools:

Central action:

2. Write Out the Ritual

Statement of intent:

Invocations/ritual elements:

3. Record Action Taken

Date/time/place, other people involved:

Additional desired information (weather, moon phase/sign, and so on):

Immediate report (how it felt, how it went, and so on):

4. Add Notes Regarding Changes or Future Ideas

5. Leave Space for Later Reflections and Feedback

Part Two

Create Your Grimoire

The next part of the book is yours! In the following pages you'll be able to collect your own information as you work. This is where you can record your rituals, divinations, spells and their results, and build on the information from Part One.

Recording your practice is a valuable tool for spiritual development. Not only can you review older material and see how your process has evolved, but you can also track specific trends and various topics that engaged you at different times. Reviewing also allows you to understand how certain aspects of your practice have fallen out of use, enabling you to either rediscover them or formally choose to let them go. Enjoy the journey!